PRAISE FOR SLEEP

C000015534

The number of caring people providing resourc *deconstructing their faith is increasing, and u s a goou ining! 1 myself provide* *resources for people as if they are pioneers searching for their own spiritual home* *where they can build the kind of spiritual life they want to live beyond the dead* *orthodoxy they once inhabited. This 40-day devotional will be added to my list of* *suggestions for those wanting a daily contemplative companion on their* *deconstruction journeys. It will help lighten their path.*

David Hayword, aka 'nakedpastor', cartoonist, artist, and author of
Questions are the Answer, and other titles

For those deconstructing from rigid forms of Christianity that remain attuned to *Christian language and metaphor, Suzanne DeWitt Hall's devotional prompts* *invite the reader to consider a more expansive, inclusive, and mysterious* *spirituality—written with gentleness and empathy for the messy and human realities* *of deconstruction in mind.*

Blake Chastain (he/him/his), host of the Exvangelical and Powers &
Principalities podcasts and writer of *The Post-Evangelical Post* newsletter

Suzanne Dewitt-Hall has done it again. Sleeper, Awake *will do just that,* *awaken you to the veracity of what you were taught to be true, to a fresh, enlivened* *paradigm of holy faith. These are 40 days of springs of living water for those who* *are deconstructing and moving towards a more radical love for Jesus. I need these* *sanctified pages more than ever.*

Cheryl M. Lyle, M.A. Bible, Transformational Life Coach,
founder: ReCONNECT Revolution

Permission granted to question your faith! An excellent companion (resource) to *walk with you on your journey of deconstructing your faith and moving toward a* *reconstruction! The devotional has guided questions and reflections that help* *overcome fears and assist in obtaining a truer understanding of who you believe* *God is in this world. A book that helps you reimagine God's kindom on earth!*

Jennifer Stephens (she/her/hers), Holy Imaginer, Inclusive Faith
Community-Cincinnati, and Faith and Religion Chair
for HRC-Greater Cincinnati

Sleeper, Awake *is truly balm to the soul. For those who are just beginning a deconstruction journey to those who have been traveling a long time, DeWitt Hall's words are filled with grace, understanding, and hope. This book is a gift to the church.*

Rev. Leigh Benish (she/her/hers),
Minister of Word and Sacrament, PC (USA)

I am constantly meeting people of faith who, like me, are pilgrims on the road of deconstruction. We are re-evaluating the long-held convictions we've inherited. Some of us are eager to embrace a more vibrant, inclusive, and progressive faith, but most of us just want to break free from something that feels like confinement. As freeing as this process can be, it can also be terrifying. How precious, then, to know that there are companions out there to help and support us on the journey. Suzanne DeWitt Hall is one of those companions. Her wisdom in Sleeper, Awake *is a gracious gift, offered in love, from one pilgrim to many others.*

Rev. Junia Joplin, Associate Pastor,
Metropolitan Community Church of Toronto

Deconstruction is usually a lonely process and involves a disconnection from relationships as we find new ways of thinking, believing, and doing that don't fit within our original religious community. Sleeper, Awake *places itself as a companion on that journey, and that's exactly what it is. It assures someone in deconstruction that even though they may not know where they're going, they're not the first, they're not the last, and they don't go alone - and yet it doesn't attempt to define the boundaries or destination of deconstruction. The best friends are those who accompany us as we discover fully who we are without limiting what we discover. A book can be a friend, especially in isolated times, and this devotional is that kind of friend.*

Rev. Stacey Midge, Pastor, Mount Auburn Presbyterian Church

Allow this devotional to be your guide on a spiritual journey of deconstruction of harmful beliefs about God and yourself. The breadth and depth of knowledge in these devotions, the gentle and encouraging tone of the writing, and the easy-to-understand structure make this book a helpful resource for spiritual growth.

Rev. Andrew Davis

If you find yourself questioning what you have been taught about Christianity, the Bible, and what it means to follow Jesus, this book is for you. Sleeper, Awake *will guide you on a journey of theological self-discovery as you face your doubts about Church traditions and dogmas. This devotional-style resource is a powerful tool in deconstructing and examining the religious ideologies ingrained in us by centuries of Church teachings.*

Rev. Tim Schaefer, Pastor, First Baptist Church of Madison

If pressed, I would have to admit that I'm on my fourth major spiritual journey of my life. I left the spiritual tradition of my birth in my early 20's, and continue to deepen myself as a biblical scholar, Interfaith practitioner, and continue to add nature-based spiritual practices from many traditions to my life as I go deeper into the mystery of the divine. There are moments, looking back, where I can recognize the learning and growing processes of my past, regardless of how visible such growth may be. One of the things I appreciate about Suzanne DeWitt Hall's Sleeper, Awake *is the encouragement to make it through those seasons of stagnation where growth is hard to see, and the mental audio tapes of mentors and parents and others who sought to stop me from further exploration. In these pages you will find a steady companion on the well-worn path to further enlightenment, despite our tendency to stop for comfort's sake. To hers, I add my encouragement to continue, even though there may have been spiritual truths that have sustained you through your life's hardest times that no longer make sense to you today. There is more truth awaiting us on the journey.*

Rev. Will McGarvey, Pastor at East County Shared Ministry, a Presbyterian USA & UCC congregation, and Exec. Dir. of the Interfaith Council of Contra Costa County (Northern California)

This is a devotional for people who rightfully question devotion to an institution that has harmed them or the people they love. This is a book for those who haven't been able to open a Bible without feeling the scars of culture wars. This is a celebration of tearing down so something new and life-giving can grow in its place. For so many, the faith the church instilled in us, failed to live up to the liberation found in the stories we learned as children. We thought we lost our faith, but really, our faith lost us. Sleeper, Awake *takes us on a journey of discovering the paradox that questioning, doubting, and deconstructing is the way toward answers, assurance, and liberation. Throughout its history, the true church has hidden herself in the marginalized so that she might awake anew. This book isn't trying to bring us back to church, but maybe help us see that love has found a home in us all along.*

Rev. Andy Oliver, pastor of Allendale United Methodist Church
in St. Petersburg, Florida

PRAISE FOR WHERE TRUE LOVE IS DEVOTIONALS

The church has been dreadfully behind on conversations relating to understanding and embracing our transgender and gender non-conforming siblings, and even within the LGBT+ Christian movement, there have been very few resources that are focused on the needs and experiences of this important community. Suzanne DeWitt Hall's new resource Transfigured *is changing that. This devotional is full of powerful meditations and reflections for the trans* and gender queer community as they journey deeper into their own spiritual lives and calls everyone who embarks on this forty-day journey towards a posture of radical authenticity and grounding in our truest selves. I recommend this resource for every faith community that seeks to minister well to their trans* and gender non-conforming members.*

Brandan Robertson, Lead Pastor, Missiongathering San Diego, and
author of *True Inclusion: Creating Communities of Radical Embrace.*

Suzanne DeWitt Hall follows her open-hearted devotional Where True Love Is *with another collection of devotions stunning in their clarity and compassion. Her short reflections on the beauty of gender diversity—both within the spectrum of humanity, and within the self of God—offer multiple lenses for trans, genderqueer, and other non-gender-conforming people to witness their own stories in the holy books of the Christian faith. Interweaving contemporary understandings of gender with ancient biblical verses, Suzanne demonstrates how our manifold God has been continually working for the inclusion, celebration, and liberation of those too often considered "other." These forty devotions are perfect for personal meditation, or for a group study during Lent or another congregational time for self-reflection and neighborly love.*

Rev. Emmy R. Kegler, Pastor of Grace Lutheran Church, founder of the *Queer Grace Encyclopedia*, and author of *One Coin Found.*

A Theology of Desire *conveys the sensual passion of spirituality and love, and their relationship. Even though we hunger for facts, finding, and fulfillment, our experience is most often questions, seeking, and desire. Suzanne beautifully expresses the beauty of this.*

David Hayword, aka 'nakedpastor', cartoonist, artist, and author of *Questions are the Answer* and other titles.

As people of faith we must continue to unpack our sacred texts anew with every generation. Suzanne DeWitt Hall's heart beats for a Christ that is both alive and relevant in a post-Christian culture. I hope many find this book and see themselves in its words.

Timothy Kurek, author of *The Cross in the Closet.*

Suzanne's work is ideal for the committed believer as well as those still trying to sort things out. The work is full of love. Love of the Word, love for the tribe, love for others and of course love of self as we have been created. We all need affirmation. You'll find that in the pages of this devotional.

Anthony Venn-Brown, author of *A Life of Unlearning.*

I just finished Sex With God *and I want to read it again. The theology is consistent and grounded, linked to interesting and surprising quotes from Pope Benedict or Rainer Maria Rilke to Marilyn Monroe and Donna Summers. The theology of Sacred Sexuality opens a dialogue long held captive by the Church. How does the most intimate act we share with others reflect the intimacy of our relationship with the Divine? And how does a healthy, wholistic sexual theology better help us to understand a healthy, wholistic relationship with our God, ourselves and our world? This book begins that journey.*

Rev. Dr. Rob Apgar-Taylor, Sr. Pastor, Grace United Church of Christ.

A Theology of Desire *is precisely that: a devotional about the sacredness of intimacy (yes, even—and especially—the physical kind). The book invites the reader to contemplate intimacy and sexuality in a way that is fresh, while remaining deeply connected to ancient understandings of Scripture, Trinity, and humanity.*

Steve Austin, author of Hiding in the Pews, Catching Your Breath, and
Self Care for the Wounded Soul.

Sleeper, Awake

40 days of companionship for the deconstruction process

The Path of Unlearning: Book One

SLEEPER, AWAKE

40 days of companionship for the deconstruction process

SUZANNE DEWITT HALL

Foreword by Rev. Joshua Noah, M.Div., M.A.

THE PATH OF UNLEARNING: BOOK ONE

Bible passages included in this book are from the World English Bible unless otherwise indicated.

DH Strategies

First Edition

ISBN-13: 978-1-7347427-3-2

Printed in the United States of America

DEDICATION

Our shared faith brought my beloved and I together initially and has been the central strand around which our cord of love has woven in the decade since. That faith has changed shapes and will undoubtedly continue to do so until our hearts no longer beat, and we experience the next grand adventure together.

This book is a reflection of our shifting and is—as always—for Dolce.

CONTENTS

FOREWORD

When I first met Suzanne and her spouse DM, I was their pastor, and was about to undergo a major phase of deconstruction as I finally accepted who God created me to be and came out as a gay man after 18 years of marriage to a woman and three kids. While my congregation was less than accepting of my God-given, deconstructed identity, Suzanne and DM were there for us when so few others were. In this devotional, Suzanne (with DM as her companion and constant inspiration) is there for you too as you navigate the spiritual, emotional, and even social challenges which come with religious deconstruction.

As a pastor and teacher, I continually undergo deconstruction and walk many people through it; from middle-aged men to teenagers. Deconstruction can be a lonely process because we're often afraid to share feelings of doubt with others, especially those seen as religious leaders or pillars of faith. During my time as an adjunct professor for world religions in the rural, conservative community where I previously pastored, well over half my students experienced spiritual famine despite the powerful religious institutions and influences prominently dotting the landscape. For many of those students, I was the first religious figure who listened to their questions and doubts without righteous judgment or superficial answers. Instead, I encouraged them by giving them more questions, acknowledging the pain of the process, and assuring them that faith is a journey, not a point of arrival. Throughout all those moments of deconstruction—both of my own and of others—I wished there was a resource that would act as loving guide through all the doubt and anxiety, all the mystery and darkness, and all the pleasure and pain.

Now I have one.

This book is simultaneously familiar yet unfamiliar. Suzanne composes a devotional that offers those who have been part of a more rigid religious structure a familiar format with which to approach time with the Divine. However, the book is also unfamiliar in that it interweaves questions and ideas that more conservative religious institutions would avoid or squash. With a gentle, pastoral manner, Suzanne walks alongside those who are deconstructing through possible roadblocks and traffic jams they may experience along the journey: spiritual abuse, emotional grief, fearful uncertainty, institutional backlash, abandonment by God, and even the loss of Jesus. She names and acknowledges these anxieties—along with the spiritual and emotional pain that comes with them—while gently nudging the seeker back on the path toward deepening mystery and greater unknowing. By the end, though the process is far from over, the reader is left with the epiphany that the opposite of faith isn't doubt. The opposite of faith is certainty.

For those who find it heretical to question God, the Scriptures, or the Church, I remind you to read your Church History. Suzanne's writing is in line with great mystics of the Church who posed the same challenging questions about doubt and uncertainty in works such as St. John of the Cross's *Dark Night of the Soul*, Julian of Norwich's *Revelations of Divine Love*, and the anonymous *Cloud of Unknowing*. We also see such questioning and deconstructive theology in the work of modern-day theologians such as Paul Tillich, Richard Rohr, John D. Caputo, and Peter Rollins. Suzanne's writing is faithful to the history of the development of Christian theology; especially as we enter the Great Emergence. She has taken complicated and frightening theological questions from throughout the history of the Church, brought them into the 21st century, and formed them into a devotional with all the pastoral love and guidance we deserve during a time of such upheaval as deconstruction. What is so heretical about that?

If the Church wishes to remain relevant and necessary to people's lives in the age of the Great Emergence, then the Church—along with all its pastors, leaders, members, etc. —has to be willing to address questions and doubts without being defensive and derivative. The entire Church needs to be honest about the fact that we all have doubts and questions. That we are all wrestling with deconstruction at some level. We need to stop trying to be something we're not. For if there's one thing people seek in a world of social media superficiality and influencer fakery, it is authenticity and vulnerability. Any church/congregation/faith group that is willing to embrace authenticity and vulnerability becomes a microcosm of the Beloved Community within their little corner of God's creation. And this devotional is a tool to help them do that. This is the devotional for the Great Emergence.

If you still think lifting up such doubts and questions will lead to the death of the Church, then I would question your faith. I never worry about the Church dying, because in Christianity, we worship a God who refuses to stay in the grave. Perhaps what you're actually witnessing is the Church resurrecting into something new, and you're unable to recognize the resurrected Body of Christ among you.

May your deconstruction journey be filled with struggle, pain, and darkness so that you may experience a deeper and more meaningful sense of peace, joy, and light.

AMEN (So. Be. It.),

Rev. Joshua Noah, M.Div., M.A.
Minister of Word & Sacrament: Presbyterian Church (USA)
Pastor: Open Table United Church of Christ, Mobile, AL

INTRODUCTION

Teach thy tongue to say "I do not know," and thou shalt progress.
Maimonides

The fact that you're reading this book implies that the tenets and mechanics of your faith can no longer be accepted without scrutiny. Several things may have contributed to this new reality. You or a loved one might have come out as LGBTQIA+, forcing you to re-examine what it means to be Christian. The socio-political climate might have brought you face to face with hypocrisy. Or perhaps you simply met someone who looked at people and God in ways you'd never encountered before. There are a thousand paths which lead to the door of questioning.

You aren't alone on the journey. A movement of unlearning is sweeping the world, resulting in casualties and new creations, heartbreak and joy, damage and freedom. The process unfolds differently for everyone, so you'll find parts of this book apply to you while others don't. As you turn the pages, you'll encounter passages from Christian and Hebrew Scripture, thoughts from Christian mystics, and quotes from a variety of faith traditions. Part of the process of deconstruction is recognizing that truth cannot be constrained within a single religion and can be found outside and inside them all.

As you move through the process of deconstruction, you'll face crossroads of despairing or going deeper, sometimes more than once. Some people halt when their carefully assembled structure of faith collapses, taking relationships and ways of life with it, deciding they'll never be duped like that again, and demanding there's no such thing as divine truth. I hope you aren't in that place, but if you are, I'm praying for you as I type these words. May the Spirit whisper into the depth of your soul that while the details of the faith you held may have been wrong, it doesn't mean God isn't still breathing life into creation, and pumping love throughout your being with every beat of your heart.

Deconstruction is hard, freeing, painful, life-affirming work. May this book provide comfort and companionship as you walk through it.

DIVINE PRONOUNS

As my years of unlearning have unfolded, my language has evolved as well. I've abandoned the idea of a solely male deity and envision instead a God who is neither male *nor* female, while simultaneously both male *and* female as explained in the Genesis creation accounts. You will therefore find the following pronouns used throughout the book:

Creator/Father   They/Them/Theirs

Jesus   He/Him/His

Holy Spirit   She/Her/Hers

DECONSTRUCTION BASICS

In this section we'll take a look at what deconstruction is, how it begins, and other basics about the path of unlearning.

DAY 1: WHAT IS DECONSTRUCTION?

Here's the Merriam-Webster dictionary definition for deconstruction:

The analytic examination of something (such as a theory) often in order to reveal its inadequacy.

Christian deconstruction is a process of questioning what was previously unquestioned and grappling with the implications of what's revealed as elements are stripped away. It can be kickstarted by all kinds of things, and take place about wide-ranging topics like church, faith, scripture, colonization, mission, Christian community, sexuality, gender understanding, racial justice, economic disparity, the problem of pain and suffering, or climate change and climate care.

The process of constructing our religious understanding takes place over the course of years. We learn some bits as children then more as adults, and when we embrace our faith actively those building blocks are cemented into a belief system. Deconstruction is similarly not a one-time event. For many of us it will be ongoing for the rest of our lives.

Don't let that frighten you. You might be intensely uncomfortable right now, in the throes of imagining the potential disintegration to come. But there is so much light at the end of the infinite tunnel which leads to God. Walking toward joy and fullness is participation in that joy and fullness. The discomfort will dissipate, but the joy will continue to beckon.

Following the call eventually leads to reconstructing a new thing, something less concrete and more wonder-filled, less rules-insistent and more saturated with love, less othering and more unity-building.

Construction, deconstruction, reconstruction. It's the cycle of life and the cycle of faith, and we're right here in the middle. Get ready to tear down walls and see the beauty which lies beyond them.

God is not found in the soul by adding anything, but by a process of subtraction.
Meister Eckhart

DAY 2: THE AWAKENING

The concept of awakening crosses religious traditions. Here are some words from Paul on the subject:

Awake, you who sleep, and arise from the dead, and Christ will shine on you.
(Ephesians 5:14b)

So much of life begins with an awakening. From our first confused blink in the light outside the womb, to the shock and awe of love, and eventually to the finality of death. All of these things and many more are the beginnings of new phases which result in clarity, insight, and depth of understanding.

Deconstruction also begins by being shaken awake. The increased alertness might jar like the shrieking of an alarm clock, or come gently and gradually. Regardless of how it happens, we must be wakened in order to grow.

When we rise after sleeping, we tend to be hungry. Spiritual awakening is similar, and in that stage of shifting our soul demands answers. We hunger for truth and feel driven to dig until it's found.

The divine light is waiting and watching, eager to feed us food that is nurturing and delicious, satisfying our souls.

Sleeper, awake, and be fed.

This capacity of waking up, of being aware of what is going on in your feelings, in your body, in your perceptions, in the world, is called Buddha nature, the capacity of understanding and loving.... The root-word "budh" means to wake up, to know, to understand. A person who wakes up and understands is called a Buddha. It is as simple as that. The capacity to wake up, to understand, and to love is called Buddha nature.
Thich Nhat Hanh

DAY 3: ABUSE IS A LEGITIMATE CATALYST

Some people begin questioning faith and church after experiencing abuse. The shift can take place immediately or can unfold years afterward. If that's happened to you, people might say you shouldn't let a single bad situation poison you to Christianity.

The Black Lives Matter movement isn't simply about individual cases of police violence captured on video. It's about a systemic problem which is finally gaining national attention. The same thing is true with sexual abuse in churches, and sexual assault in the workplace. It's been there for generations, and people are increasingly talking about it. The abuse you received through a church, friend, family member, or authority figure is not an isolated incident. There's not just a single bad apple, there's an orchard full and harvest time has come.

Questioning structures which permit abuse is appropriate and necessary. Questioning the individual people and situations involved in your own abuse is warranted. If those questions lead you to analyzing your faith in a broader sense, it's a good thing and leads to healing; for you and for the broken systems themselves.

It's natural for us to associate the divine with hurts perpetuated or supported by the church, but God and religion are not the same thing. The one who is Love is pleased when you deconstruct after being harmed. They want so much more for you than the wrongs you've received.

You are allowed to unlearn every narrative that has kept you shamed and small.
Aundi Kolber

DAY 4: THE GIFT OF DISCONTENT

The idea of contentment is sometimes promoted as a Christian virtue, perhaps based on Paul's writings to the Philippians. He's far from alone in the idea, however. In Buddhism contentment is called "the greatest wealth," and the path of enlightenment leads to it. Sikh gurus teach contentedness as one of the Five Virtues, and the Yoga tradition also focuses on it.

In contrast, deconstruction is characterized by feeling ill-at-ease. Contemplative author James Finley calls this state "holy discontentment," and says God creates it as part of the call to more: more access, more presence, more unity, and more awareness.

Being discontented is a hint we're attached to the wrong things. The comfort we used to get from pastors, scriptures, or church services is no longer available, because they don't contain enough of what we really need.

If you're experiencing a season of discontentment, don't despair. Look for the new things God wants to reveal. Imagine the possibility of being content within the discontented place; waiting for attachment to the wrong things to fall away, creating emotional and spiritual space.

It's there, in that vacancy, where you can realize increased union with the lover of your soul.

> *Prayer, love, spirituality, and religion are about ridding yourself of illusions. When religion brings that about, that's wonderful, wonderful! When it deviates from that, it is an illness, a plague to be avoided. Once illusions have been abandoned, the heart is unobstructed, and love takes hold. That's when happiness occurs. That's when change takes place. Only then will you know who God is.*
> Anthony de Mello

DAY 5: A JOURNEY OF SELF DISCOVERY

One of the most uncomfortable aspects of deconstruction is realizing there are pieces of yourself that you don't like. It could be ways you've engaged with the world, judged others, or did nothing when you should have spoken up. The further you move away from the strictures of rigid Christianity, the more intense these feelings of regret and shame may become.

If you're experiencing shame about the way you conducted yourself based on faith beliefs, extend yourself a bit of grace and forgiveness. We can't change the past. All we can do is try to learn from our mistakes and try to not repeat them.

There is freedom in knowing you might be wrong. It relieves a lot of internal pressure, and gives others permission to seek, learn, and grow. Your humility relaxes things and halts competition. It helps people realize they don't have to try so hard, and that not having all the answers is a form of strength.

Deconstruction is a journey of discovery, and some of the most important revelations are about our very selves. Let's keep learning new things, and growing into more.

I did then what I knew how to do. Now that I know better, I do better.
Maya Angelou

DAY 6: ACKNOWLEDGING WHERE YOU ARE

Self-knowledge is critical for many things; getting to the root of emotional issues which need healing, ending up in a satisfying career, making use of the appropriate love languages when dealing with a partner, child, or other loved one, even doing basic things like managing money. Without self-awareness we don't have a foundation for how to effectively proceed. But association with churches or other faith communities can lead to a lack of self-examination. We sit in our assigned mental pews and do what is expected, even while thinking we seek God's will. The liturgy and patterns of our participation keep us from looking too closely at what's happening in the hearts, minds, and spirits of ourselves and others.

It's good to take a bit of time to contemplate where you are, pondering questions about your level of comfort with your church if you still have one, and considering the conversations about God you have, even inside your own head.

Where are you right now? Are you questioning everything you've been taught, or do you just feel discomfort about a few issues?

Are you happy in your church community or do you find yourself squirming?

Is your mind and heart being fed or are you on your own in seeking truth?

There's no single correct place to be, but being frank with ourselves is helpful, and if we don't assess we can't know.

Deconstruction is a journey, and when you're navigating your way to a new place, it's helpful to know where you're starting from.

Let us place our first step in the ascent at the bottom, presenting to ourselves the whole material world as a mirror through which we may pass over to God, the supreme Artisan.
St. Bonaventure

DAY 7: WHAT'S YOUR GOAL?

As you consider where you are in the process, it's good to ask what your goal for unlearning is. Your journey may have begun from a position of anger and resentment, particularly if you were launched into deconstruction by trauma. In these situations, the goal might be to gather evidence with which to slam those who harmed you. Perhaps you or a loved one came out as LGBTQIA+, and you want to offer a divinity-based defense of queer identity. Maybe social injustice initiated your journey, and you're searching for answers about why Christianity has shifted so far away from the message and actions of Jesus. While goals like these are understandable, I'm hoping with time your impetus transforms into something even deeper.

Deconstruction offers a path toward unmediated communion. When we're busy following the rule system of a particular faith, much of what we perceive about God is filtered, because the system itself is viewed as the proper method for experiencing God. When we step away from that system many of the filters are stripped away, and we're offered the opportunity to engage with the divine differently, and potentially, to receive more.

Our goal for unlearning should always be a search for truth. Not a way to get back at your family for forcing church on you, or an amassing of a new religiosity which is "better" than the one you're tearing down. Just truth within the limits our human brains can comprehend.

Truth shines, calls, and wants to be found. Truth is found beyond thought, beyond rules, beyond words, and beyond walls.

Let the goal of your deconstruction be truth.

> *Mysticism is the art of union with Reality.*
> Evelyn Underhill

DAY 8: DEATH TO SELF

The concept of death is frightening even when the loss isn't of life itself, but of ideas, certainty, and self-image. In the view of the divine, however, the lines between life, death, and rebirth are less distinct.

Jesus offered words of encouragement for pushing through the fear we face about dying things:

> *Most certainly I tell you, unless a grain of wheat falls into the earth and dies, it remains by itself alone. But if it dies, it bears much fruit.*
> (John 12:24)

When it comes to deconstruction, the seeds are our concepts of certainty, our sense of wisdom, and the notion that we can contain adequate knowledge of the divine. They're planted by our initial desire to know God and by the systems Christianity is so good at developing. But they're just seeds, and if we want to grow into deeper understanding, they need to perish.

The idea of death is scary, but is what happens to nascent things really death? Seeds buried in the dirt plump from exposure to water, then swell and crack as the burgeoning life inside becomes too insistent to be constrained. The seeds that once were can no longer be seen, but the new things which grow from them are varied and beautiful.

We fear death more than anything else, but it's simply part of an ongoing transformation. Our certainty must die, but it is a death by love. And it's required if we want to experience the exquisite new things which bud in its place.

> *When he shall die,*
> *Take him and cut him out in little stars,*
> *And he will make the face of heaven so fine*
> *That all the world will be in love with night*
> *And pay no worship to the garish sun.*
> William Shakespeare

DAY 9: STAGES OF LOSS AND MOURNING

Deconstruction includes lots of loss, so there's a good chance you'll go through some of the stages of grief. Let's take a look at what they are:

Denial: When first struck with the reality that something important is no longer in our life the human brain doesn't want to believe it. In deconstruction, we can putter along asking new questions and having doubts, and then suddenly realize we're losing things. When loss finally hits, our denial can be strong enough to put deconstruction on hold. But once the door to questions is opened, it's hard to shut it again, and the reality of our need to continue searching tends to resurface.

Guilt: Most of our faith is built on the shoulders of important people in our lives. They might be parents, youth pastors, beloved priests, Sunday school teachers, or others. As we face the loss of our understanding of Christianity, guilt may rise up. You might feel guilty about the people who instructed you, and you might feel guilty about God.

Anger: As you evaluate decisions you've made and actions you've taken because of your faith, you may experience irritation and anger. You can be angry at the centuries of tradition which shaped the denomination which formed you, angry at those who were formative of your faith, angry that life used to be simpler, and angry about feeling misled. You might be angry at yourself for having accepted things you now find unacceptable and doing things you now regret. You can even be angry at God for permitting the whole thing to happen.

Bargaining: As you grapple with loss you might try to make deals with yourself or the divine: "If you make X happen, Lord, I'll do Y." If you find yourself doing this, acknowledge that it's a coping mechanism, and try not to hold yourself too tightly to these internal agreements.

Depression: Feelings of depression are logical as you experience losses related to deconstruction. Please seek help if you have difficulty pulling out from them.

Acceptance: While the initial phases of deconstruction can be highly anxiety producing, acceptance eventually comes, bearing with it a measure of peace.

Reconstruction: As you move through the phases of grief and continue opening yourself to the things God wants you to see, hear, and experience, you'll begin to re-form your understanding of the divine, and envision how your life will reflect this new understanding.

The stages of your grief process might not take place in the order listed above. They might overlap, or you could experience some but not all of them. Please know that you are not alone, and remember that it will get better. Hope and joy await.

In sorrow we must go, but not in despair. Behold! We are not bound for ever to the circles of the world, and beyond them is more than memory.
J.R.R. Tolkien

Our Fears

Over the next few days we'll address fears you may encounter. Facing them head on might not rid you of distress entirely, but hopefully it will reduce the pressure to a manageable level so you can move forward.

Day 10: Fear of Uncertainty

As part of a church, community, or family in which the members hold all the same faith views, we tend not to question what we're taught. The closed circuit creates confirmation bias, where messaging from the outside is filtered by the group's belief system. It's only when we venture outside that we recognize inconsistencies, logic problems, and hypocrisy.

Seeing those cracks can make us uncertain and fearful. But Jesus taught using parables which befuddled his cultural contemporaries and remain confusing today.

Christianity has transformed from The Way of following God through the teachings of Jesus into a demand for certainty and correct thinking. Letting go of certainty is uncomfortable. But the watery image of God we see through a glass dimly is far from accurate and demanding otherwise means missing out on experiencing the divine in a deeper way.

Certainty ends thought, dismisses questions, and halts further reasoning. Uncertainty invites searching and permits growth.

God makes room for ambiguity and knows there is power in uncertainty. It's scary, but it's the only way to get to more.

No despair of ours can alter the reality of things, nor stain the joy of the cosmic dance, which is always there.
Thomas Merton

DAY 11: FEAR THAT RELIGIOUS EXPERIENCES WERE FALSE

Christian traditions differ in their focus on *experiencing* God. Worship music in contemporary Evangelical settings is timed to evoke emotion during various parts of the service. Charismatic and Pentecostal churches emphasize physical encounters, sometimes even pressuring congregants into speaking in tongues or being slain in the spirit. Taizé prayer can carry participants into a Zen-like meditative state. You may have had physical responses like these as you've sought God, and you might be worried that those mountain top experiences weren't real.

But what if the opposite was true? What if they contained more truth than the belief system constructed by your faith journey? What if these encounters are glimpses into the grandness which lies beyond the constraints our religious foundations enforce?

If you've been trying to explain away mystical or ecstatic encounters with the divine as mere emotional manipulation or blips in brain chemistry, give yourself permission to stop. Let those experiences simply exist for now. Maybe even return to them periodically and remember how they felt.

We live in a universe of extraordinary wonders. Don't be too quick to dismiss the experiential miracles in your own life. Allow the wonder to exist. If your deconstruction eventually results in atheism or nihilism, it will harm nothing. And if it unfolds into increasing layers of mystery and awe, you can recall them as doorways to what awaited.

When we exhaust our human-based problem-solving designs, God emerges and shows us the way forward.
Dr. Jacinta Mpalyenkana, Ph.D, MBA

DAY 12: FEAR ABOUT WHAT GOD WILL THINK

The questions which blossom throughout the course of your unlearning can come fast and furious, or creep in over longer periods of time. Regardless of how quickly the process unfolds, eventually you'll face a profound fear:

What will God think about your questions and doubts? If God is the creator of the universe and the sustainer of your very breath, how dare you question what they require for holiness?

This fear reminds me of the culminating scene in the Wizard of Oz. Our intimidating image of God is actually a little man with a blustery voice amplified into an angry, controlling deity who demands sacrifice. But God is larger than any man-sized concept, and our human-shaped idea of justice as equivalent to rage is similarly false, constraining, and reductive.

So much of what Christianity has become today is man-made, just as it was when Jesus walked the earth and pointed out hypocrisy and abuse. It's no simple process to sort through what is good, true, useful, and beautiful, and what is human-inspired and inaccurate. But a God who is love will not be angered by someone wanting to focus on the former and reject the latter.

God is love, truth, connectedness, and life. They could never be mad at you for seeking truth, for that is who they are.

Listen to yourself and in that quietude you might hear the voice of God.
Maya Angelou

DAY 13: FEAR OF DISORDER

Toddlers have two joys when playing with building blocks. The first is stacking them up. The second is knocking them down.

We tend to associate order and structure with reliability and truth, and messiness with a lack of credibility. But all existence sprang from chaos and darkness. From the diaspora the good news spread. In the fetid darkness of rot, seedlings spring into life.

Blocks wouldn't be fun if they couldn't be tumbled into a pile of promise on the floor. There can be no eureka moments if the pieces are cemented into a monolith rather than remaining free to be formed and reformed.

As kids get older, they begin experimenting with the different ways pieces can be combined, trying to see how tall they can stack a tower, how beautiful a building can be when assembled from blocks of varying colors, or how balance works when making a bridge. If we permit the pieces of our spiritual structures to tumble in heaps around us, we have the opportunity to rearrange the pieces and see what results.

If you're feeling fearful about the jumbled state of your faith, remember that disorder doesn't last. We can't get to new things if we cling to the existing order. From chaos comes life.

Ruin is a gift. Ruin is the road to transformation.
Elizabeth Gilbert

DAY 14: FEAR OF LAWLESSNESS

As a new believer I was offered several analogies for why Christian rules are so important. One was a question: how is a train most fully itself? The answer: when it remains on its tracks. The other was the image of children playing in a fenced-in playground next to a forest, safe from the dangers in the shadows beyond the chain-link.

If you were taught this idea, it's understandable that you might worry what could happen if Christianity as we know it crumbles. You might even wonder if your own sense of right and wrong will vanish leaving you vulnerable to new temptation.

But non-Christian cultures all over the globe create communities which haven't devolved into chaos and anarchy. Millions of atheists lead extremely ethical lives.

Can fences protect the vulnerable? Yes. But the people inside miss out on the wonders of ferns, moss, and berries, of dappled shade and the sound of creatures rustling through fallen leaves. Does a train operate best on its tracks? Yes. But the places they travel are limited, and there are vast lands waiting to be explored, full of adventure, new relationships, and deepening wisdom.

Discarding rules proclaimed by Christian denominations will not result in you or society running amok. It's possible that the new ethical system which evolves as a result of widespread deconstruction will be richer, more robust, and more socially just than what we see today.

Be at peace, and keep going.

One of the greatest needs of humanity today is to transcend the cultural limitations of the great religions and to find a wisdom, a philosophy, which can reconcile their differences and reveal the unity which underlies all their diversities.
Bede Griffiths

DAY 15: FEAR OF NOT KNOWING WHAT TO DO

Some phases of the deconstruction process feel manageable. Your foot is on the gas pedal and the car is driving along at a pace which allows you to look out the windows, marveling at the sights passing by, and anticipating a future of enlightenment.

But unlearning strips away the certainty of right action, and we're faced with expanses of time when we aren't sure what to do next. The car you thought *you* were driving suddenly takes on a life of its own and an unseen foot pushes harder on the gas. You may want to stop but it's not possible because the mass of what you've already realized has gained too much momentum. There are no brakes.

At that moment, you won't know what to do. That's a scary state.

When you truly can't control something, the best course is often to simply let what's happening happen. It's a bit like steering into a skid when you're driving on ice. Instinct screams to slam on the brakes and jerk the wheel in the other direction. But the only way to avoid catastrophe is to stop trying to control it and let the forward motion carry you through.

Not knowing what to do can be scary, but it permits things to happen which otherwise couldn't, and it can save you from doing the wrong thing and crashing.

When you feel panicked and unsure about what to do next in your journey of unlearning, take your hands off the wheel, release the pressure from the pedal, and breathe.

Enlightenment is really nothing more than just no longer believing your own thinking.
Adyashanti

DAY 16: FEAR THE CHURCH WILL CRUMBLE

I'm a people pleaser and really good at harboring guilt. Hopefully you aren't like that, but in case you are, there's a chance your worries about deconstruction include what could happen to your church without you. This is particularly true for clergy, but also occurs for people who do a lot of volunteering.

The truth is that it's not your responsibility to hold everything together. Even if you're the pastor. Even if you're in charge of the kids. Even if you're the church secretary who keeps the place running like a well-oiled machine. Unless you helped found it, the church you attend existed before you came through the door, and most likely will carry on for some time to come. And if it crumbles, it will be due to reasons extending far beyond the role you played.

You might also wonder what widespread deconstruction's impact will be on Christianity as a whole. I'll say it again: it's not your responsibility to hold everything together. Given the ubiquitous problems within Christianity, reform needs to happen. While that's underway churches may close, denominations may shrink, and Christian colleges may shut down. But if churches hide abuse, denominations ignore Jesus' call to social justice, and colleges use scripture as a weapon for exclusion, is it really a bad thing if they close their doors?

Christianity has survived 2,000+ years, and the structures developed in the name of the Christ will rise and fall regardless of whether we remain within them.

You aren't powerful enough to destroy any of it.

What I know now is that the church of Jesus to which I was devoted will survive into the future, no matter what I do or say. Nothing I do will impair the vehicle's ability to do good, or its ability to do damage. Every large-brained hairless primate in the church will continue to minister according to their god-given spiritual instincts. As individuals, if we primates find that the ideology of our tribe of origin, or some members of our tribe, are interfering too much with our spiritual instinct packages, we eventually move on. There comes a point where we can no longer tolerate the smell of their urine, which covers every bush and tree in the territory. We need to find a tribe where we like the smell. This one-by-one exodus from the many orthodoxies of Christianity has been going on for centuries. Assuming we survive as a species, that exodus will continue for many more centuries.

Ronald Goetz

DAY 17: FEAR OF LOSING ETERNITY

Christians hold varying views of what comes after our time roaming the earth. Visions of heaven include gold-bricked roads with winged singing figures, life-flowing rivers with shorelines covered in fruit and medicinal plants, and lions and lambs frolicking together. Hell might be a place of burning torment, a banquet table with seven-foot-long forks, or simply a continuation of humanity's lack of compassion. But most of us believe *something* happens after death. We're taught that our faith, our actions, or some combination of both will decide our final destination.

Fear of death has been a tool of control from humanity's early days. The concept of simply ending is terrifying for many (perhaps most) of us, and so the people and institutions seen as holding the keys to what happens after death wield power. Those who provide a set of rules for ensuring eternal pleasures are magnetic, and we circle them seeking assurance that our ideas of good and bad are correct, and that there are achievable formulas for ensuring we end up in paradise.

But what if our concepts of righteousness-based damnation or reward are wrong? How do we endure the idea that there may not be an eternity in the way church has proclaimed it?

It helps to acknowledge that each cell in our body is built from atoms which are spinning particles of energy, because energy can't be created or destroyed; it's merely transferred or changes forms. This means our existence continues, even after our hearts stop beating and our brains stop processing signals. In a very tangible way, our life force carries on after death. Our transformation into pure energy removes all the filters to perception that our bodies inflict, and all the barriers to union with other things that our bound molecules enforce.

Maybe some essential us-ness will remain at that point and we'll be permitted to explore the universe in a sentient way, investigating mysteries we wondered about on earth. Or maybe our very essence will be freed to interact with different parts of the universe in new ways, perhaps scattering so we become one with the grasses, insects, and trees. Perhaps eventually burning, our heat rising, pushing particles

22

high into the air, then drawing moisture to become rain drops, eventually watering the earth. Maybe we'll be like the divine, knowing and experiencing all these things as they happen, all at once.

We can't know what comes after our existence in the glorious burden of our bodies. But we know that existence does continue in some manner. We can believe there is a throbbing power of love beating at the center of all things, and hope that the design for what comes next is equally glorious. We can let go of the fear and angst of hellfire and damnation, and the idea that any of us is good enough for a good-boy-based heaven or bad enough for an eternity of fire.

And we can ponder the wonder of dissolving into oneness with the Creator and creation.

You can't lose eternity. You're already in it.

Human beings need not despair and go on an eternal search for the Eternal, for the Eternal has come to the temporal.
Steve Kumar

DAY 18: FEAR OF LOSING JESUS

Deconstruction inevitably leads to examining beliefs about the Christ, which can be particularly frightening given the central tenet of Jesus as savior and mediator. But do we need to be afraid of losing our ideas of him in those roles? Let's hear from Jesus himself on this topic, as he chats with a Samaritan woman:

> *Jesus answered her, "Everyone who drinks of this water will thirst again, but whoever drinks of the water that I will give him will never thirst again; but the water that I will give him will become in him a well of water springing up to eternal life."*
> (John 4:13-14)

The scene is rife with meaning. It takes place at Jacob's well which acts as a symbol for the old, venerated ways of doing things. The woman represents things which the formal religion of Jesus' milieu condemned. She was part of a culture which didn't worship God in the "right" ways. She'd had many husbands and now lived with a man who was not one.

The woman asks worried questions about whether it was okay to worship God on the mountain where they talked, or if it could only happen in Jerusalem. Jesus clarifies that the old ways of thinking about worship were over.

His words offer comfort for us today. Like that woman, we're offered the living water of a larger God. Sipping it can result in a fountain of yearning which reaches beyond the strictures of organized religion.

You may lose the idea that Jesus was the lamb which a blood-thirsty deity demanded be sacrificed on the altar of his rage. Your concept of his divinity may wane and wax as the years unfold. You might also choose to enter into a search for Christ as the pulsing force of love through which all things came into being. All of these variants are acceptable with the divine One who created you to think, question, and thirst for truth.

The Christ isn't a megalomaniac who demands undivided focus. Jesus doesn't care if our thirst for more leads us to look around, behind, and through him as a doorway. He pointed at the one he called Abba and said a Spirit would be our consoler and comforter.

Jesus doesn't want you to simply swallow what your faith formation offers, and let it grow still and fetid. He's completely okay with the places the well of living water takes you. God themselves offers it.

Enlightenment, for a wave in the ocean, is the moment the wave realizes it is water. When we realize we are not separate, but a part of the huge ocean of everything, we become enlightened. We realize this through practice, and we remain awake and aware of this through more practice.
Thich Nhat Hanh

DAY 19: FEAR OF LOSING GOD

Awakening to increasing levels of truth is a very good thing, but it's a deeply vulnerable condition with an enormous fear lurking in the shadows. Your heart may be skittering around it even now:

"What if I lose God?"

As you continue your awakening, there may be stretches of time in which you aren't sure you believe in God anymore. You might be angry and disillusioned enough to consider the whole thing a farce. Your experiences and phases of grief can impact the duration of this state.

The dark night of the soul is no joke. It's a frightening condition which saints throughout the ages experienced. Depending on your trauma level, you may need to lose God for a while, maybe even through the end of your life. If that happens you'll be in extremely good company. Mother Teresa of Calcutta suffered with it for 50 years.

Just don't overestimate your power. Even while awake our ability to comprehend reality is limited by our sense organs and brain capacity. What you believe or don't believe about the divine doesn't change the reality of their existence.

You may lose God, but God will never lose you.

The transition from innocence to knowledge is always perilous and fraught
with hazard. There is something very comforting and reassuring about
innocence. To dwell in innocence is to inhabit a region where storms do not
come and where all the breezes are gentle and balmy. It is to live in the
calm of the eye of the hurricane. It is to live in a static environment which
makes upon the individual no demands other than to be. All else is cared
for; is guaranteed.
Howard Thurman

CONSIDERING GOD

As you unpack aspects of your belief system, the rock is still there, waiting for your touch. In this section we'll take a look at the God which Christianity attempts to contain.

Day 20: God Is Love

Many people think Jesus claimed divinity by saying that seeing him meant seeing the Father. While this focus is understandable given Christianity's dependence on Jesus as God enfleshed, it misses what might be even more important.

The people of Jesus' culture had very specific concepts about God and requirements for righteousness, but even then the faith was not one thing. Pharisees and Sadducees argued about issues as profound as whether or not there is resurrection after death. The people of Samaria worshipped the same God but disagreed on where sacrifices should take place.

Despite this diversity of belief, many aspects of understanding about God were essentially the same, and most didn't align with the image Jesus presented. Jesus was born into humanity. He disrespected the Sabbath and violated laws related to defilement. He hung out with despised people and sinners. And ultimately, he was murdered.

This is a profound and scandalous thing. How could the God of rules for righteousness break them? How could the author of creation die?

God is bigger than the Jesus story, and *that* story was earth-shaking. The divine seems to like pointing out that our views of who and what they are will always be wrong.

God is love, burning with desire and creation. Burning with desire for you, and your neighbor, and the robin pecking for worms, and the worms, and the bacteria feasting in the dirt consumed and eliminated by the worms, and the atoms making up the bacterial cells, and the subatomic particles making up those atoms.

God is the essence of a love so grand it exists even when we attempt to kill it. Love, powering the universe, and calling to you now, through these words.

Love, which might be called the attraction of all things toward all things, is a universal language and underlying energy that keeps showing itself despite our best efforts to resist it. It is so simple that it is hard to teach in words, yet we all know it when we see it.
Richard Rohr

DAY 21: SEEKING IS FINDING

Faith has been described as a dance of beckoning and responding, with the divine hand extended toward us first. The invitation is always and eternally offered, while the offeror patiently waits. Meanwhile, we thrash and crash through life, trying to figure out what we believe, and sometimes questioning whether it makes sense to search for answers at all.

But our minds are incredible meaning-seeking machines designed to not simply look for answers but to be hungry for the questions themselves. There is satisfaction in the hunger. Let's look at these words from Matthew's gospel:

> *For everyone who asks receives. He who seeks finds. To him who knocks*
> *it will be opened.*
> (Matthew 7:8)

In seeking there is finding. The existence of longing implies that satisfaction awaits.

C.S. Lewis expounded on this idea, telling us that the experience of hunger is proof that food exists. The fact that we are cold tells us there is warmth, waiting somewhere, to embrace us. And the fact that we yearn to know the deep forces which power the universe is assurance that there is a marvelous momentum which enlivens it all.

Your questions do not threaten the existence of God. The quest is an experience of the finding.

> *There is pleasure in the pathless woods.*
> Lord Byron

DAY 22: JESUS TALKED WITH US

You may or may not believe Jesus is fully God and fully human, but it's interesting to contemplate what God might hope to accomplish by appearing in human form. One potential is they wanted to talk to us.

In prayer we send up our concerns, dreams, and praises, occasionally perceiving some message being returned. But by taking human form, God could walk among us and state things we needed to hear directly.

At the time of Jesus' birth, the prevalent notion of the divine will being all about rules and regulations meant we sorely needed a talking to. Jesus arrived and offered correction in the form of conversation, instruction, and calls to action.

But Jesus didn't simply preach, he also listened. He never minded queries except when used as snares by the chief priests and scribes. His apostles asked questions, and the crowds who followed him did too.

Jesus wasn't afraid of questions at that turbulent moment when people's faith was turned on its head and everything they'd thought they knew about righteousness was disrupted. There was great fruitfulness in their digging.

Rich work takes place in the ask and answer. God wants to talk with us.

Prayer belongs to everyone: to men and women of every religion, and probably even to those who profess no religion. Prayer is born within the secrecy of our being, in that interior place that spiritual writers often call the "heart".
Pope Francis

DAY 23: JESUS CAN BECOME AN IDOL

The idea that Jesus can become an idol is likely to be labeled nonsensical or heretical by those who call themselves Christian. If this is your reaction, stick with me for a few minutes to explore the possibility.

The eternal question of why evil exists is explained in religions around the world through stories of counterbalancing gods of darkness and light. Christianity offers a variation of the concept by presenting two distinct deities: the jealous, vengeful god who thirsts for blood in appeasement of his anger, and the sacrificial savior god who offers himself to satiate that thirst. Our insistence that Jesus is the stand-in for millions of sacrificed pigeons, goats, and oxen fetishizes him into a totem figure in the shape of a slaughtered lamb. The hyper focus on his death and resurrection has become a shoddy graven image of the Creator's magnificence.

When we stop perseverating about Jesus as sacrifice for our sins, we realize he is a role model for unlearning. He released a tsunami of faith deconstruction, constantly preached rethinking, and castigated those who made stringent demands about righteousness through rule following.

The first person to encounter the resurrected Christ was Mary Magdalene, a woman who was so intimate with Jesus that she kissed his feet. When he appeared in the garden outside his tomb, Mary tried to hold on to him but Jesus pushed away her clinging.

That message is for all of us. The man Mary Magdalene perceived wasn't the full truth of his being. By letting go of a Jesus she understood, trusted, and loved, Mary Magdalene was able to embrace something much more profound. When we stop clinging to an idolized Christmas/Easter Christ and seek deeper universal resonance and meaning, we can also experience a relationship beyond our imagining.

Let's all set down the Jesus idol, and look deeper.

If God created us in his own image, we have more than reciprocated.
Voltaire

DAY 24: GOD IS WHERE THE MORE IS

Jesus presents the idea of Love coming in "lesser" form to show us they are more. He offers an image of human divinity so magnetic that he draws people away from lives and loved ones, from safety and certainty, and from the understanding of our own righteousness. He did it back then, and he's calling to you and I to do it now.

Jesus shows us a divine human who is the very force of gravity, inviting us into wonder about what else we don't know. Telling us we're foolish to think our conceptions could possibly be correct.

God is where the more is.

The Alpha and Omega whisper to us about being life and light, and of the call from and to love. Whispering that we are more, and that we are one.

God is where the more is.

The divine whispers to the place within you which aches with questions and hungers to be filled. God is the endless filling of that endless ache in an endless parade of souls filling the universe.

The divine can never be contained or constrained, it can only be sought. Our searching should strip away anything which keeps God small so we can reach for the more.

God is where the more is.

If we comprehend it, it is not God
St. Augustine

DAY 25: GOD IS NOT CONTAINED BY ANY RELIGION

There's a good chance your Christian training taught you to be suspicious of other religions. Your denomination may even believe that other faiths are satanic, and that the followers of those traditions will burn in hell. The missionary zeal many Christians feel is often fueled by those beliefs, creating problems across the world through actions of colonization. The view contributes to radicalization against people of other religions, leading to discrimination, marginalization, and hate crimes.

The Roman Catholic Church has tried to shift away from this kind of thinking, with official statements emerging from the Second Vatican Council in the 1960s, and Pope Francis' more recent urgings that Catholics shouldn't be afraid of religions other than Christianity. The Greek Orthodox Church has made similar formal statements, like this one:

Orthodoxy recognizes and accepts the mandate to seek Truth and to follow the Holy Spirit wherever He leads, including in other religions or philosophies when his Truth is to be found there.

These are powerfully important words for people steeped in structured views of Christianity. But they're also critical for those of us who are deconstructing our faith, a process which is all about the effort to strip away falsehood and seek truth.

Don't be afraid to explore different religions and spiritual approaches. God is found in them, and God's desire is for ever-increasing closeness with you, culminating in an ultimate, eternal union.

Wherever you find truth which leads you toward intimacy with the divine and with the rest of humanity, God is there, and God is pleased.

The great treasure that interreligious dialogue among the world religions could unlock is to enable people to get to know and love other religions and the people who practice them.
Thomas Keating

DAY 26: GOD OF ABANDONMENT

Today we consider words Jesus cried from the cross:

> *"Eloi, Eloi, lama sabachthani?" which is, being interpreted, "My God,*
> *my God, why have you forsaken me?"*
> (Mark 15:34b)

Jesus expresses the pain of abandonment even though Christianity teaches he was fully God and unable to be separated from the divine. The concept of Trinity means he was always accompanied, and never alone. But in those final excruciating moments, Jesus appeared to experience abandonment. Deconstruction may lead you to feeling similarly alone, adrift in uncertainty and pain, hungry for answers, and mourning what has been lost.

Reciting the first line of a Psalm was a common method for referencing the passage and offered a way of communicating its full context. Jesus' cry was a reference to the opening verse of Psalm 22:

> *My God, my God, why have you forsaken me?*
> *Why are you so far from helping me, and from the words of my groaning?*

Let's read on:

> *But you brought me out of the womb.*
> *You made me trust while at my mother's breasts.*
> *I was thrown on you from my mother's womb.*
> *You are my God since my mother bore me.*
> *I am poured out like water.*
> *All my bones are out of joint.*
> *My heart is like wax.*
> *It is melted within me.*
> *My strength is dried up like a potsherd.*
> *My tongue sticks to the roof of my mouth.*
> *You have brought me into the dust of death.*
> (Psalm 22:9-10, 14-15)

Our pain in deconstruction can be palpable. In many cases our faith was formed at our mother's breast. We can't understand how something which seemed so solid can quiver anxiously or even crumble. We know God *could* rescue us from the uncertainty if they wanted to, and don't understand why they won't.

The psalm is full of pain, but it ends in promise and comfort:

> *You who fear Yahweh, praise him!*
> *All you descendants of Jacob, glorify him!*
> *Stand in awe of him, all you descendants of Israel!*
> *For he has not despised nor abhorred the affliction of the afflicted,*
> *Neither has he hidden his face from him;*
> *but when he cried to him, he heard.*
> (Psalm 22:23-24)

Jesus referenced the Psalm so the hearers would understand both the pain and the comfort of a God who abandons and yet never abandons. A God who appeared to be far from the body on the cross and yet was still and always there.

It might be hard for you to see the divine face right now or in days to come. But God is there, watching, listening, and hearing you when you cry out. The God who abandons you will never actually abandon you.

Even if you abandon them.

> *in time of all sweet things beyond*
> *whatever mind may comprehend,*
> *remember seek (forgetting find)*
> *and in a mystery to be*
> *(when time from time shall set us free)*
> *forgetting me, remember me*
> E.E. Cummings

36

DAY 27: GOD OF ABANDON

Yesterday we talked about the idea of God abandoning us. Today we look at the root word "abandon," and consider the power of opening ourselves to various forms of abandoning.

Google's first definition of the term is to leave something empty or uninhabited, without intending to return. In deconstruction, we often leave churches and religious groups when we realize our thinking is no longer consistent with theirs.

Another definition is to release someone or something to a particular fate by no longer trying to change them. In deconstruction, we resign ourselves to the reality that people we love aren't going to be with us on the journey we're undertaking.

The term can also mean to give up a course of action, practice, or way of thinking. This is what unlearning is inherently about.

Jesus told his followers to lay down their fishing nets, ignore the burying of their dead fathers, and leave their very lives behind. He recognized the loss but promised they would gain much in return. His words are truth which extends beyond the decision of the disciples who chose to follow him: in all endeavors, things must be left behind before we can move forward.

There's one more meaning associated with abandon: to allow oneself to indulge in a desire or impulse. People abandon themselves to music, passion, or the first bite of chocolate cake. In deconstruction, we must relinquish our tight reins of control, and release ourselves into the experience. This, above all, is what God wants from our journey of unlearning: abandonment to what may come.

The burning desire of the divine is for you to enter fully into searching for and with them. God wants us to seek them with reckless abandon, not ignoring the losses incurred, but not being stopped by them either.

Enter into abandon, and savor the promise your creator offers in return.

Deep within us all there is an amazing inner sanctuary of the soul, a holy place, a Divine Center, a speaking Voice, to which we may continually return. Eternity is at our hearts, pressing upon our time-torn lives, warming us with intimations of an astounding destiny, calling us home unto Itself. Yielding to these persuasions, gladly committing ourselves in body and soul, utterly and completely, to the Light Within, is the beginning of true life. It is a dynamic center, a creative Life that presses to birth within us. It is a Light Within that illumines the face of God and casts new shadows and new glories upon the human face. It is a seed stirring to life if we do not choke it.
Thomas Kelly

DAY 28: THE CLOUD OF UNKNOWING

Pseudo-Dionysius the Areopagite was a 5th to 6th century Christian philosopher who wrote extensively about God. He describes two opposing approaches for understanding the divine. The first method is described as *kataphatic* which refers to the way we assign characteristics to the Godhead. For example, Christians might say God is loving, just, good, jealous, and all powerful. Contemporary evangelical Christianity tends to be kataphatic in theological approach, claiming God is knowable and definable. All one must do is memorize the Bible and you've essentially eaten God and can poop out righteousness.

The second approach the philosopher describes is *apophatic* which maintains we can't comprehend God because of their transcendence, and so all descriptions must necessarily be what the divine is *not*. For example, they are not knowable, not containable, and not finite. The idea that we can't ever know God but can only love them and rest in the absence of certainty was termed "the cloud of unknowing" by another ancient author, this one who chose anonymity.

Contemplative Christianity embraces the apophatic methodology, freeing us from the demands of our minds to *know* through information. It invites insight which is experienced rather than understood, the way you realize new levels of intimacy with a partner through lovemaking rather than conversation.

We are programmed to be uncomfortable in states of uncertainty. But there is a deep knowing which can only come from love, and not from study.

Deconstruction is the invitation to enter the intimate cloud of unknowing.

> *The first time you practice contemplation, you'll only experience a darkness, like a cloud of unknowing [which now happily envelops you]. You won't know what this is [and will have to learn how to live there by "forgetting" your previous methods of knowing]. You'll only know that in your will you feel a simple reaching out to God. You must also know that this darkness and this cloud will always be between you and your God, whatever you do…. God is incomprehensible to the intellect… Nobody's mind is powerful enough to grasp who God is. We can only know God by experiencing God's love….*
> *God can be loved, but not thought.*
> From *The Cloud of Unknowing*, author unknown

ENCOURAGEMENT FOR THE JOURNEY

Our final focus area offers words of encouragement for your process of unlearning.

DAY 29: THINGS MIGHT GET BUMPY

As a baby matures in the womb, it eventually can't get enough of what it needs through the umbilical cord. Our lungs were made for air. The baby isn't happy about the process, but it has to get out. Imagine the pain involved: the squeezing of contractions, being forced to change shape, ejecting from the safety of a warm place, and the shocking discovery that the womb wasn't the totality of the universe. The deconstruction process is similar. We feel out of control, thrust where we don't want to be, in a place that feels cold, glaring, and somehow empty.

Babies scream their fear and outrage at the violation of their safety. They wail as they are wiped clean, weighed, measured, and have their capabilities tested. Once those tasks are complete, they're returned to the embrace of their mothers where their cries are soothed. It's a new embrace, which must initially feel less intimate, and certainly feels less safe. But being outside is the only way for the relationship to continue to develop and deepen.

It's hard to know how long the terrors and trauma will accompany your own birthing into a wider, more expansive world, and an eventual deeper relationship with the one who delivers you. It could be brief, taking just a few weeks, or it might be drawn out. Babies in the birth canal sometimes stop making progress, and your own forward momentum may stall or reverse. Your thoughts and emotions will hit peaks and valleys. There's a very real chance you'll experience anxiety, depression, or a sense of meaninglessness during some phase of unlearning. Pay attention. Tell others how you are feeling. Seek help. You might even need medication temporarily, and if you do, that's okay. Things will get better.

The process of being born is messy and frightening. But oh, the marvels you will see as you toddle through a new, wider, world.

It is not impermanence that makes us suffer. What makes us suffer is wanting things to be permanent when they are not.
Thich Nhat Hanh

DAY 30: A GREAT CLOUD OF WITNESSES

While the faith journey often begins in community and is fed, formed, and nourished within it, each of us must face the "God issue" individually. It's an intensely intimate undertaking, perhaps the most intimate of all: just you and the author of creation coming to grips with how your relationship will proceed.

It can be a lonely space, but in those moments of loneliness, try to remember you aren't actually alone in the process of unlearning. The movement to reject limits on God is taking place across denominations and geographical boundaries.

Imagine for a moment that *you* are the one being searched for. Imagine if all those you loved cast off false impressions about you, and sought you earnestly with questions about what the truth might actually mean. How would you feel knowing a tsunami of beloveds were seeking to find you, to know you better, to love you without barriers?

I can only imagine how gloriously happy the creator must be that all this is happening.

You are a participant in that great cloud of humanity—past, present, and future—whose hearts yearn for more while fumbling through the details and questions. You're not alone, and your questions have meaning.

The process of deconstruction must be engaged in individually, each of us grappling with our unique history and the individual wonderings of our hearts and minds. But there's a cosmic quest underway, a consequential work of global magnitude.

And you're part of it.

The sound of the genuine is flowing through you... Cultivate the discipline of listening to the sound of the genuine in yourself.
Howard Thurman

Day 31: Be Kind to Yourself

I've repeated a few concepts as we've moved through this book. Spaced repetition is a technique for consolidating ideas into longer-term learning, and issues of self-care during deconstruction are important enough to warrant internalization.

Deconstruction hurts. While it will be punctuated with moments of hope and joy from glimpses of truth and beauty, it contains loss, anger, fear, and other negative emotions. You'll be tempted to deride yourself for your past views, or your current emotion. You may feel like you can't be trusted to know right from wrong, truth from lies, or sweet hope from propaganda.

To move forward, you need to experience all these feelings. Ignoring them or pretending they don't exist just sublimates emotion and delays progress. But as you allow the feelings, try to be gracious with yourself. Imagine yourself as a young child who suddenly discovered Santa Claus was actually your mom, dad, or caregiver. A time of transition is needed for the child to realize there is new depth and wonder in discovering a parent created all that magic.

Should the child be judged for their previous belief?

Of course not.

Take it easy on yourself. Be aware that your body plays a role in processing deconstruction trauma and try to be good to it. Drink water. Rest. Take walks. Breathe fresh air. Seek beauty.

Hug that inner child who feels deceived and discouraged. Remind them that the real magic is deeper, more complex, and endlessly worthy of exploration.

Talk to yourself like you would to someone you love.
Brené Brown

DAY 32: BECOME WHO YOU ARE

As you move through the deconstruction process, you'll transform in ways which might surprise you. Allow yourself to consider a few questions:

- Who are you, inside?
- Who do you *want* to be, both interiorly and in action?
- What gets in the way of you becoming those things more fully?

Shedding the constraints which faith traditions so often link to right relationship with God not only opens the door to deeper revelation, it also changes your understanding of self. At first this may feel like an identity crisis. But the earth explodes with effulgent diversity. Creation writhes with ever-changing life, endlessly evolving into new variations in an ongoing effort to be more.

It's clear that the designer adores change.

Constraining ourselves is like growing watermelons in square boxes. The melons are uniform, which make them easy to transport and store, but they never get to be what they were made to be; full and curving into different shapes and sizes. Unique, irregular, and ill-fitted to mass handling.

You are a creation born of divinity, and a bearer of it. Your changing and ongoing becoming can never be problematic for the God who dreamed you into being.

The more *you* you are, the more pleased they will be.

Be who God meant you to be and you will set the world on fire.
St. Catherine of Siena

DAY 33: GROW COMFORTABLE BEING ANSWERLESS

Humans like ready answers, and the more complex the problem we can answer, the more comforted we feel. It's an evolutionarily useful trait, because unknown plants, animals, and situations can be dangerous. Knowing the rules keeps us out of trouble.

Certainty feels safe and so we tend to associate it with God, but rule systems come with boundaries and procedures which vary widely across time and culture. This means there are always groups of people operating outside the realm of "rightness," but the divine burns with desire that we might all be one; with each other and with them. Creating separation is anti-Christ.

The need to feel like we know more than we actually do is a spiritual pitfall. It hurries us to answers and solutions rather than lingering with the discomfort of waiting. And hurrying leads to embracing concepts even when they conflict with our deep values, or simply don't make sense.

It can be uncomfortable to admit that you don't know who or what God is and how best to live a holy life, even to yourself. But would you rather feel confident that you are right, or feel open to wonder, mystery, and love?

If your unknowing leads to a widening concept of God, and a more deeply felt understanding of the intrinsic value of others, isn't it worth the discomfort?

To be able to say that your faith is superior, you also have to have a faith that provides all the answers. And therein lies the problem with toxic Christianity, it tries to prove superiority by offering answers it doesn't have; and in doing so, it kills faith by claiming certainty.
Jo Luehmann

DAY 34: WRITE YOUR OWN CREED

Churches all around the world recite creeds proclaiming basic tenets of belief about Christ's coming. The Nicene Creed and the Apostles' Creed are familiar examples. Formal statements like these were typically developed during unsettled times to declare an "official" stance for what constitutes orthodox belief. For example, the Athanasian Creed was designed to distinguish "true" faith from the heresy of Arianism.

My friend Cheryl Lyle has a master's degree in biblical studies and was formerly a pastor in The Salvation Army. She's been deconstructing her faith for years, and posted these thoughts on what she currently believes:

I don't believe God is anything other than wonder and mystery. I don't believe the Bible is the inerrant Word of God but rather I can experience the wonder and mystery of God through the words of scripture. I believe God is more than three co-equals. There is much more to God in character. I believe religion is how we live out our experience with wonder and mystery in caring for others. I believe faith is how you define your values and morals. This is me Becoming.

While Cheryl didn't intentionally write a creed, that's essentially what this thought stream is. Putting it into words helped her shape the new thing her exploration is creating. The word "Becoming" at its conclusion is especially powerful, because it indicates her understanding is dynamic and unfolding. The statement isn't a static thing which she'll proclaim from now until the earth explodes as it draws too near the sun. It's an ongoing blossoming.

As you walk through deconstruction, consider writing your own creed which presents the bare bones of your belief. You might find it a useful exercise for capturing this moment in your own becoming.

Until every soul is freely permitted to investigate every book, and creed, and dogma for itself, the world cannot be free. Mankind will be enslaved until there is mental grandeur enough to allow each man to have his thought and say.
Robert G. Ingersoll

DAY 35: MYSTERY IS GOOD

We've talked a fair bit about the need to let go of certainty if we want to know God with deeper intimacy, and we're talking about it again today. Our discomfort with ambiguity is such a persistent thing we need regular reminders that the unknown is actually a *good* space to explore.

C.S. Lewis included this familiar snippet of dialog in *The Lion, the Witch, and the Wardrobe*, speaking about God as represented by Aslan:

> *"Is he—quite safe? I shall feel rather nervous about meeting a lion."*
> *"That you will, dearie, and no mistake," said Mrs Beaver. "If there's anyone who can appear before Aslan without their knees knocking, they're either braver than most or else just silly."*
> *"Then he isn't safe?" said Lucy.*
> *"Safe?" said Mr Beaver; "don't you hear what Mrs Beaver tells you? Who said anything about safe? 'Course he isn't safe. But he's good."*

Many forms of Christianity claim memorizing Hebrew and Christian scripture, reciting pre-processed theological takes, and avoiding a specific set of behaviors gives us favor with God. Contemporary Christian reading of Paul's writings exemplifies this tendency. His letters include numerous mystical nuggets but legions of Christians focus instead on rules and regulations outlined for young churches. It's much easier to focus on practical things than on the mysterious bits.

The situation reminds me of Gnosticism. The term comes from the Greek word gnôsis, meaning "knowledge" or "insight," and while the ancient Gnostics held a variety of beliefs which contradict contemporary Christian thought, the idea of access to special knowledge is markedly in play.

When considering the vastness of space, the depths of the sea, or the mystery of the human brain, we easily recognize that we know much less than we don't know about each of these places. So how can we possibly comprehend the vastness of God?

The reality is that when it comes to the divine, there are countless more questions than answers. Acknowledging our unknowing gives us a chance to seek for more, despite the discomfort.

Like C.S. Lewis's lion, mystery may not feel safe, but it is good.

What we know is a drop. What we do not know is an ocean.
Sir Isaac Newton

DAY 36: MANSION UPON MANSION

16th century mystic St. Teresa of Avila's autobiography *The Interior Castle* describes the soul's journey toward God as a series of seven mansions, each one a state of faith, practice, and experience of the divine.

The concept of places in which to be sheltered and grown is also found in the gospels. In John 14:2, Jesus assures the apostles gathered at the last supper that his father's house had many homes, rooms, mansions, or dwelling places (depending on your preferred translation.)

There is no single "right" faith place. In life, people change houses, moving across town or continents. Moving can be scary, and the work of it exhausting. But there are things to be learned and enjoyed in each and every house, even if the one you're in now feels empty and echoing. The house is made of love, and we are permitted to abide in it for however long is needed.

There are many ways to access God, and many ways to dwell with the divine. The varying phases of our individual faith journeys are all nooks in which to meet God, as are beliefs found in different religions. They are all spaces to dwell with love, and be fed, nurtured, and grown.

We are mansions in which God chooses to dwell, and you contain the heaven they wish to bring to life here on earth. All our phases of deconstruction and reconstruction are temporary. A final destination of endless unfolding awaits.

The gate of heaven is everywhere.
Thomas Merton

DAY 37: LET GOD BE BIGGER

St. John of the Cross wrote about our ideas of God getting in the way of our union with them, and explained that it's only in the empty darkness when those notions are stripped away that we can finally come closer. Deconstruction starts us on that path of stripping away. The dark night of the soul creates space which becomes available for filling, for encounter, even for wonder at what thrumming presence might inhabit the dimness.

When we let God be bigger than the constraints religion imposes and open ourselves to being ravished by this truth, we're given a particular kind of freedom. Acknowledging and embracing our lack of understanding frees us from preoccupation with ourselves. There is pain in losing the idea of divinity we've clung to. The loss of concreteness can be piercing, and may cause us to wonder if God exists at all.

But God is bigger.

The divine indwelling makes every bit of matter intrinsically valuable, and their transcendence renders all matter inherently insignificant. Both things are somehow fully true. Both things are fully contradictory. Your views about the sacred are both incredibly important and meaningless. Both things are also true and contradictory.

The pulsing reality of God is bigger than our ideas of God can ever be. Step into the space of unknowing. Release your ideas. Encounter a presence in the absence.

Let God be bigger.

God does not die on the day when we cease to believe in a personal deity, but we die on the day when our lives cease to be illumined by the steady radiance, renewed daily, of a wonder, the source of which is beyond all reason.
Dag Hammarskjöld

DAY 38: UNION AS THE DIVINE TRUTH

Our brains filter out huge quantities of sensory input so we can focus on the tasks closest at hand. It's a necessary function because the world is so full of sensory data that if they didn't it would be extremely hard to focus on getting a fire started or detecting whether a mushroom is the kind that nourishes or poisons. We simply aren't capable of processing too many things simultaneously.

This reality impacts our existence on every level. We're physically wired to focus on ourselves, our needs, and our thoughts, and that self-focus can be blinding. In our faith lives, we unconsciously apply this habit of limiting input so we can be decisive and transform mystery into actionable concepts. But expanding our focus beyond self and senses opens us to wider truths.

The law of attraction is everywhere; in the gravity which holds our feet to the ground, in the adhesion and cohesion which prevents wine from spilling over the rim of a glass which you tipsily pour just a tiny bit too full, in the pull of the tides and the moon circling the earth, and in the spinning bits of energy which make up your fingernail. Our senses are so narrow we can only see the worry of bills, rules, and aging skin. But these things mask the deep truth which hides beyond our observation.

Union is that divine truth; the union of atoms to make molecules, and molecules to make substances, and stars to make galaxies, and souls to make love. The beating heart of union drives and powers the universe, and is the ultimate, undeniable truth.

The spiritual life… proceeds directly by a change of consciousness, a change from the ordinary consciousness, ignorant and separated from its true self and from God, to a greater consciousness in which one finds one's true being and comes first into direct and living contact and then into union with the Divine. For the spiritual seeker this change of consciousness is the one thing he seeks and nothing else matters.
Śrī Aurobindo

DAY 39: IT ALL COMES DOWN TO CHOICE

No amount of science or reason can establish that God isn't real, because it's not possible to prove that things don't exist. Science can ascertain that some things aren't *present* in varying situations, for example, tests can reveal that a water sample doesn't contain lead. But lead as a substance exists, separate from that sample. By contrast, astrophysics can't demonstrate that life forms don't thrive in places not yet explored. It's just impossible to prove.

This reality means that all faith comes down to choosing whether or not to believe. Once we reach an age where we can question and ponder the depths of what Christianity submits, we choose. Every day that you experienced a profoundly steady belief in God you were *choosing* to do so, even if it felt more like a forgone conclusion, or just what you are supposed to do, or even an experiential reality. But in all these cases, a decision was being made, and a "yes" was required.

We are all faced with two paths. Each of us must do the seeking to determine which path to take, and whether to knock on the door which lies midway along it. This choice is a daily occurrence. You may find your position wavering as time passes, some days dwelling in the warmth of certainty about the love permeating everything around and within you, other days feeling cold and abandoned. But each day, every day, we choose what we're going to believe. We've all been given that great gift of freedom.

Whether we like it or not, believing in God all comes down to choice. The decision is entirely in your hands.

Beyond rational and critical thinking, we need to be called again. This can lead to the discovery of a "second naïveté," which is a return to the joy of our first naïveté, but now totally new, inclusive, and mature thinking.
Paul Ricœur

DAY 40: THE CYCLE OF RESURRECTION

Deconstruction can feel like prolonged stages of death. So many pieces of our lives disappear, and things we thought previously are dismissed out of existence. Entire ways of considering reality are blinked away. The death of our faith as we know it is painful.

But resurrection is the pattern of the universe. Stars are born, collapse, and die, providing energy which forms the matter of creation. The decomposition of old things transforms into new life, life more beautiful, fresh, and filled with promise than the things which passed away. The vibrant greens of spring are unique to that season. Once they harden into the colors of summer, they aren't repeated again until the next year. Our own lives begin and progress, we become old and frail, eventually dimming and yearning for an end while new babies are born shining the light of their own promise. Our faith grows and becomes firm, then quivers and falls, and our souls become fertile space for a new thing to come.

God is with you and I through all these phases of transformation. They are with us as we release our certainty about their existence and their demands, with us in the slow drying up of our faith, the crumbling into questions, and in the drifting down into the dirt as we watch all that we thought we knew decay.

God is there. The God we can both know and never know, the God who imagined us and created us, who inhabits us and re-forms us, ever present, ever waiting, ever hoping, ever loving us in and through each stage.

Even if you can't feel them and wonder if you ever will again, God is there, anticipating you, wanting you, ready for you.

An unseen heart, beating with love, and waiting.

From darkness and uncertainty, it waits for the Divine to be born in its own time. The process doesn't try to contain new revelation in the dry, crusty soil of old forms, but germinates each seed in the moist openness of heart, fertile and hollow like the womb, receptive and waiting. It is the qualities of Wisdom, the Mother of all—merciful, gentle, humble, nondual, holistic, benevolent—that we tenderly bear. Verdant, womb-like theology welcomes new seeds to take root. Round and hollow in imitation of divine fecundity, gestation cannot be forced; new life cannot be prescribed. We cannot change the color of the eyes, or the shape of the nose. Similarly, we cannot fashion divine self-disclosure to our own liking. Impregnated with its seed, we simply support it and watch it grow.
Beverly Lanzetta

Conclusion

We are finished with our time together, but the work is not done. I'm still on the path, and probably always will be. There will be more dark nights for my spirit, more moments of intense certainty, and more phases in which I feel like Paul rendered blind, fumbling and mourning my losses before resigning myself to the reality of the ways I've been wrong and the invitation to open my eyes and mind to the glory of a reality that is impossibly grand.

As you continue moving through the deconstruction process and into a state of openness to more, I pray you'll be able to feel truth shining, calling, drawing you near, and that this light will give you comfort and peace through times of uncertainty.

God is always coming out of a formless void into revelation. The space of emptiness is rich with anticipation, and fertile with promise.

May we remain open and receptive to the potential of more.

May we always be hungry for truth.

Printed in Great Britain
by Amazon

83548866R00047